My Room

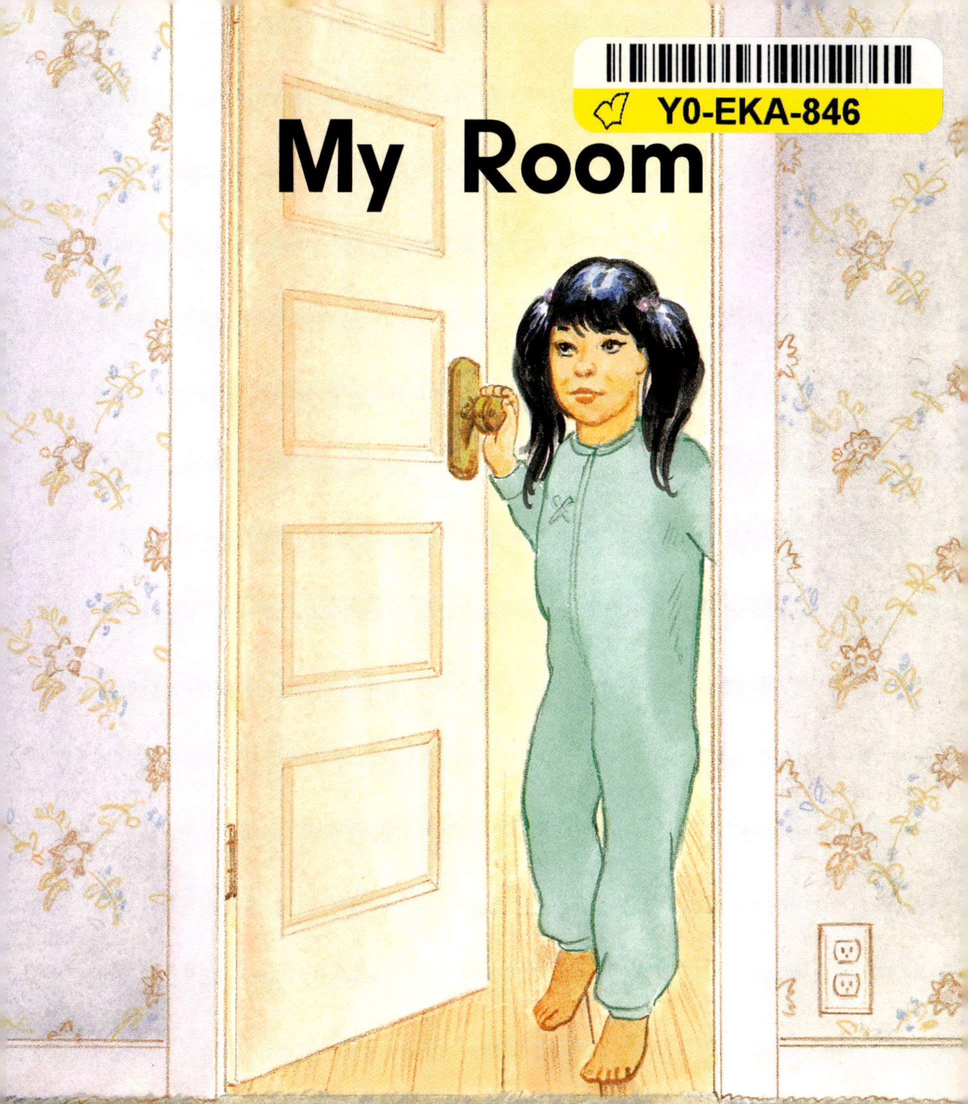

By Joe Ramsey
Illustrated by Kevin Davidson

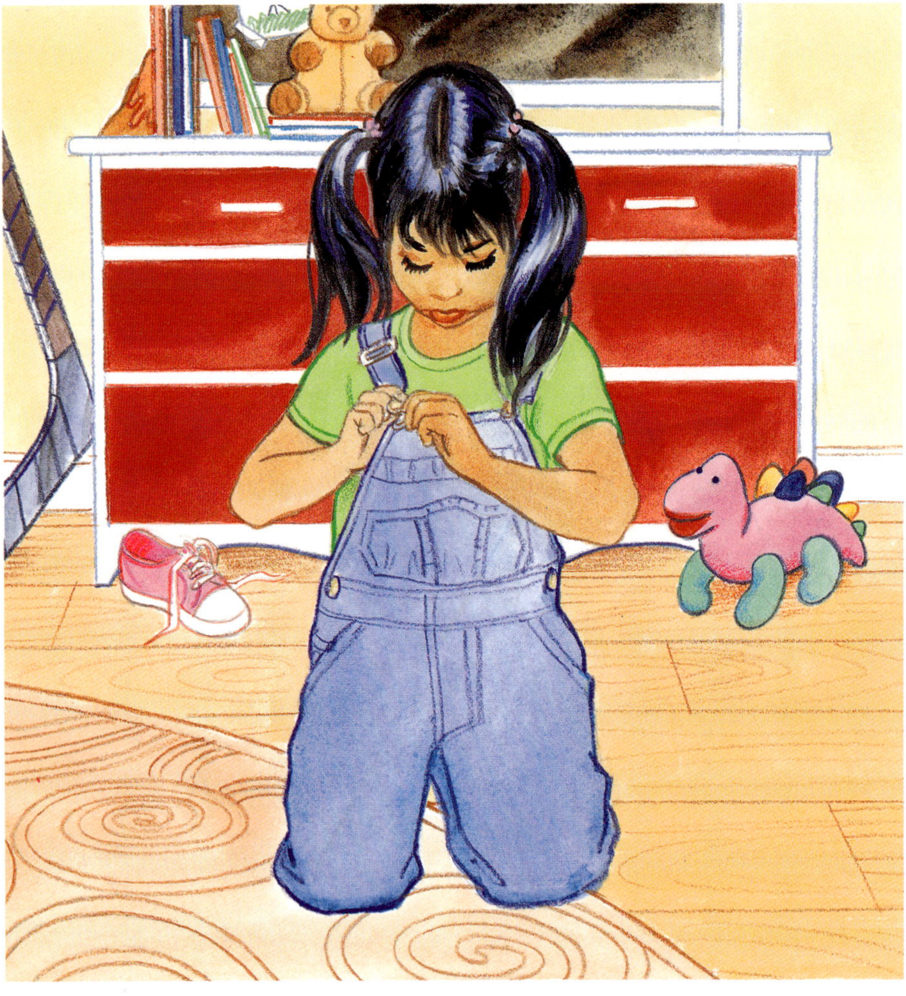

I dress.

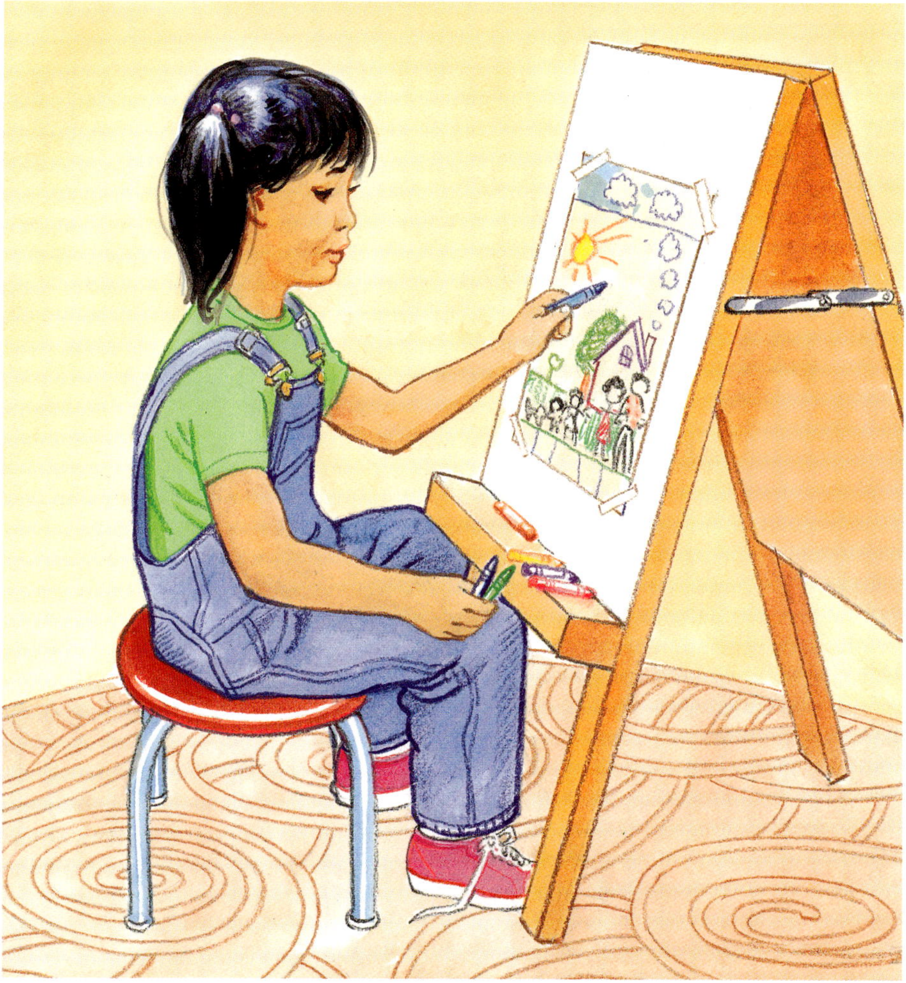

I draw.

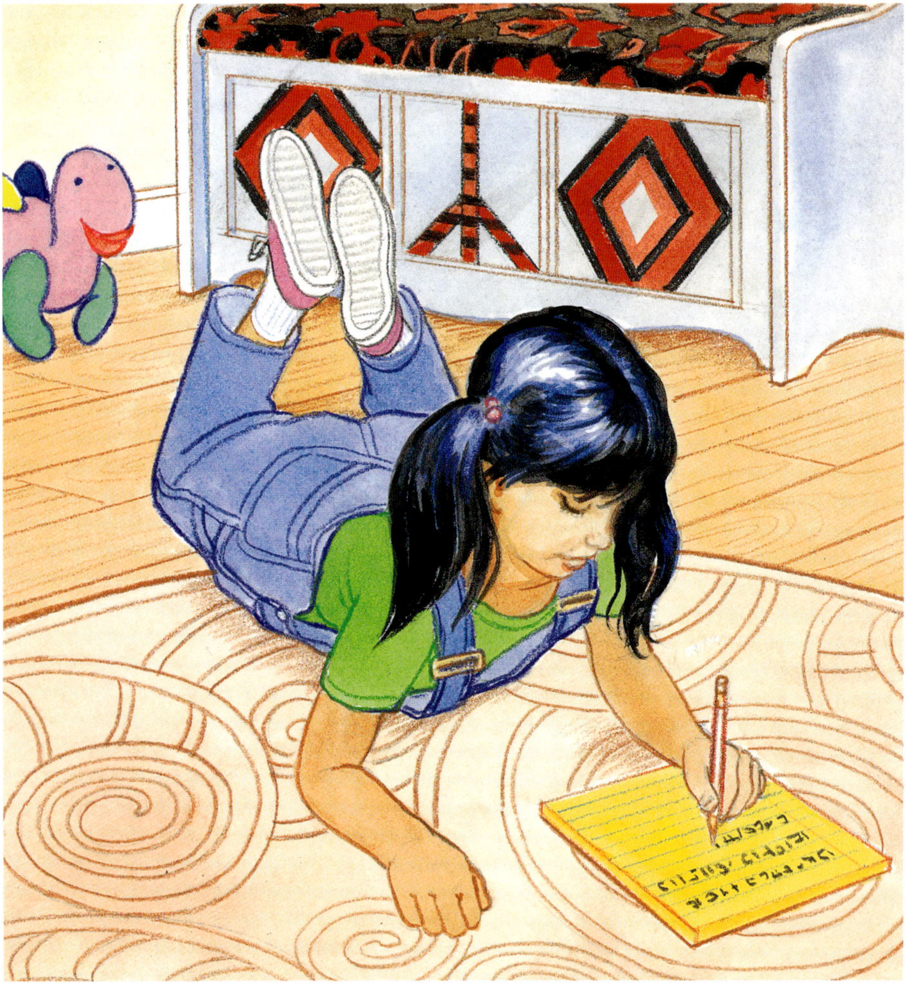

I write.

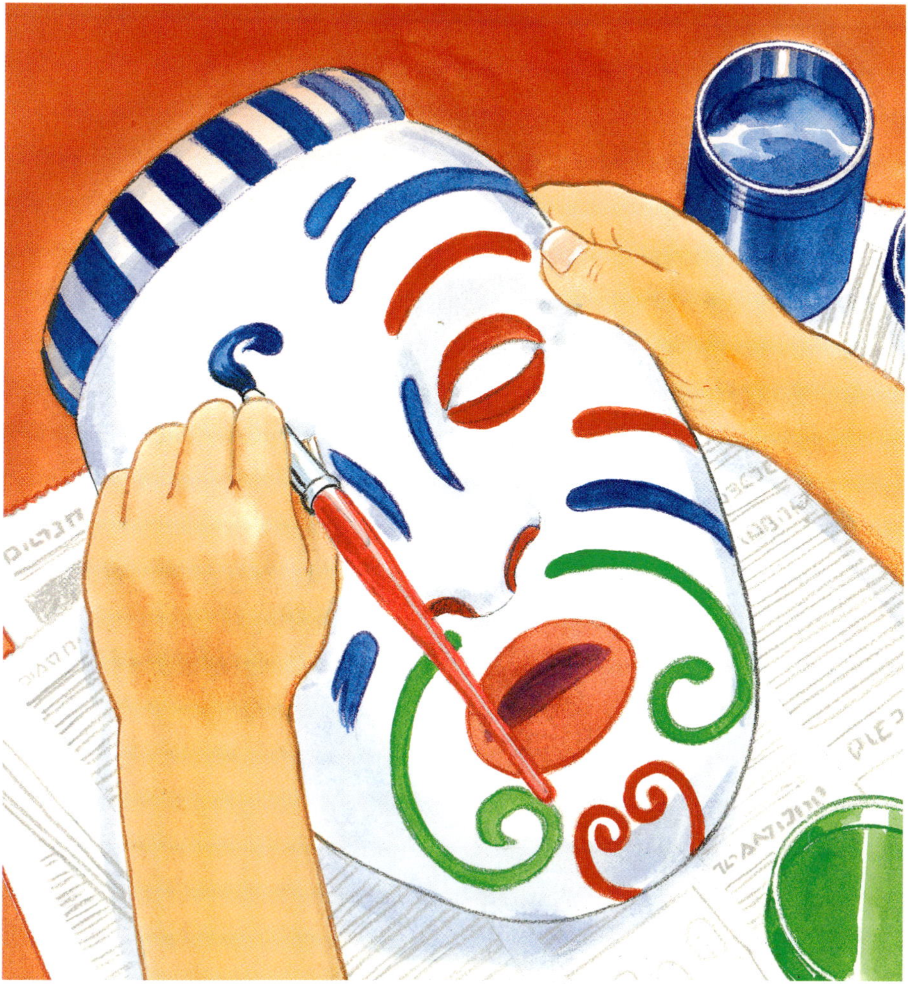

I paint.

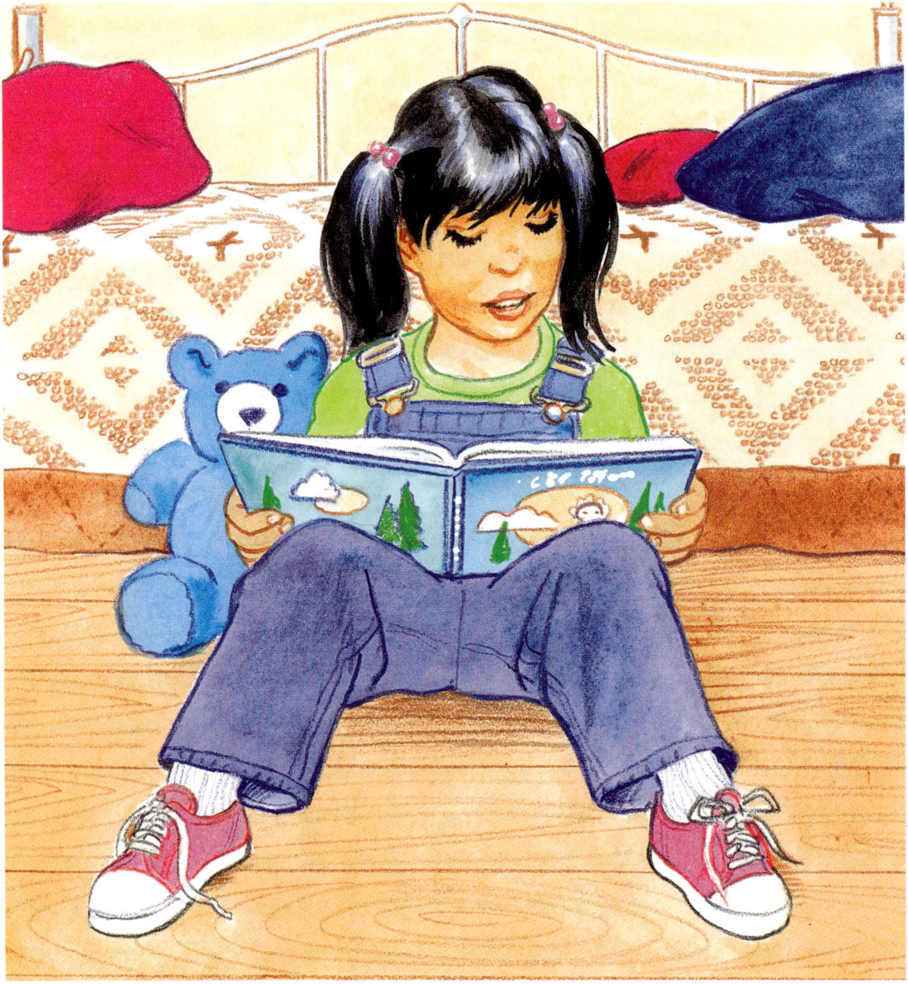

I read.

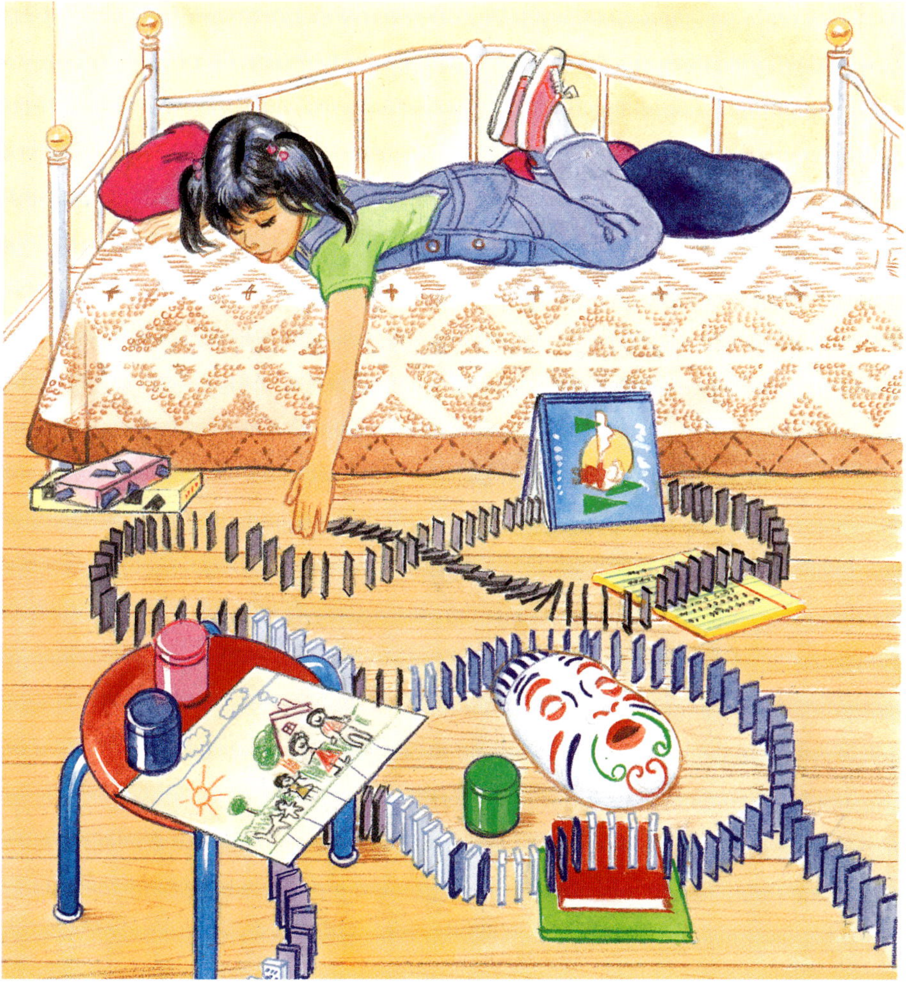

I play.

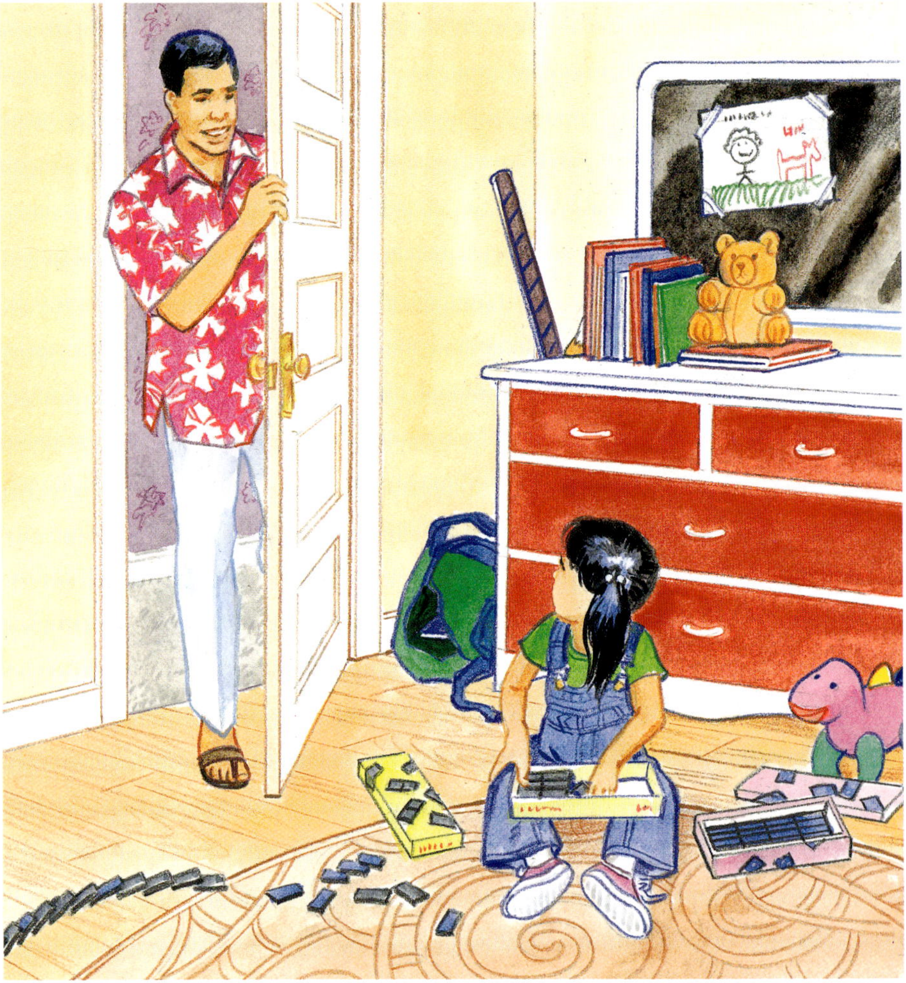

I pick up.